STARTERS

Festivals

Lynn Huggins-Cooper

First published in 2004 by Hodder Wayland,
an imprint of Hodder Children's Books,
338 Euston Road, London NW1 3BH
This edition published under license from Hodder Wayland. All rights reserved.

Text copyright © 2004 Lynn Huggins-Cooper

Language consultant: Andrew Burrell
Subject consultant: Lisa Kassapian
Design: Perry Tate Design
Picture research: Glass Onion Pictures

Published in the United States by Smart Apple Media
1980 Lookout Drive, North Mankato, Minnesota 56003

Library of Congress Cataloging-in-Publication Data

Huggins-Cooper, Lynn.
Festivals / by Lynn Huggins-Cooper.
p. cm. — (Starters)
Includes index.
ISBN 1-58340-563-1
1. Festivals—Juvenile literature. I. Title. II. Series.

GT3933.H84 2004
394.26—dc22   2004042921

9 8 7 6 5 4 3 2 1

The publishers would like to thank the following for allowing us to reproduce their
pictures in this book: Hodder Wayland Picture Library; 4, 8, 20, 21 (top), 22 /
Hutchison Picture Library; 15 / James Davis Travel Photography; 21 (bottom) /
Corbis; cover, title page, 6, 7, 8, 9 (top), 12, 13, 14, 16, 18 (bottom) / Impact; 17,
Getty Images; 18 (top) / AI Pix; 22 (top), 23 / Andes Press Agency; 9 / Zul Mukhida;
19 / Christine Osborne Pictures; 5, 10 (bottom), 11, 14 (bottom)

Contents

Party people

People all over the world love to celebrate and have festivals.

Many people celebrate their birthdays with cakes, presents, balloons, and parties.

Have you ever been to a birthday party?

During the Christmas season, many people have parties and decorate their homes. Christian people go to church to celebrate the birth of Jesus.

Beautiful decorations are hung on a Christmas tree.

5

Happy New Year!

The Chinese New Year is celebrated in February with firecrackers, lion dancers, and big paper dragons.

In September or October, Jewish people celebrate new beginnings on Rosh Hashannah.

Sweet honey cakes are eaten as a wish for a sweet year!

The Sikh New Year is called Baisakhi. It is celebrated on April 13th. In Punjab, India, people dance to music and give candy to their friends and family.

Harvest time

Christian harvest festivals celebrate the good things that God gives to people. Churches are decorated with flowers, fruits, and vegetables.

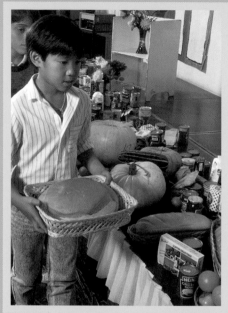

In Ghana and Nigeria, people celebrate the Yam Festival. They dress in traditional clothes and thank the gods for their food.

During the Jewish festival of Succoth, people give thanks to God for the harvest. They build special tents or huts, called *succah*, outside in the yard.

People decorate their succah with harvest foods.

Festivals of light

Hannukah is a Jewish festival that lasts eight days. To celebrate, people light a *Menorah* candle.

A new candle is lit every night.

During the festival of Holi, Hindu people throw colorful powders and water around to make everything bright.

Everyone is covered in color!

Diwali is the festival of lights celebrated by Hindu and Sikh people. People light beautiful lamps and eat special food.

Sparklers and fireworks light up the night.

Celebrating the seasons

May Day is on May 1st. It is celebrated in parts of England by people dancing with ribbons around a maypole. It celebrates springtime and how plants begin to grow.

The ribbons become tied around the pole by the dancers.

Apple Day is a fall festival. People in some countries visit orchards to taste different kinds of apples.

In the United States, people celebrate the fall harvest on Thanksgiving. Many families eat a delicious meal and give thanks.

This special turkey is decorated with seasonal fruits and herbs.

Spooky festivals

In the U.S. and Britain, Halloween is celebrated on October 31st.

Scary faces are carved into jack-o-lanterns.

Some people dress in spooky costumes. They go trick-or-treating to collect candy from people they know.

In Mexico, Dias de los Muertos is celebrated on October 31st. On that day, people remember relatives who have died.

They cook delicious meals and eat sugar skeletons and coffins!

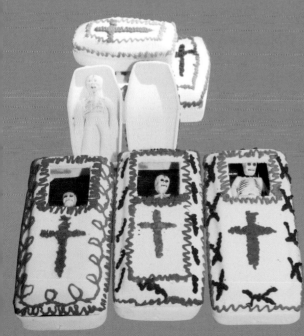

On May 5th, some Japanese families celebrate Tango-no-Sekku, the Boys' Festival.

For each son, a colorful paper fish is hung outside the house.

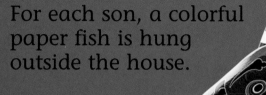

The Japanese Girls' Festival on March 3rd is called Hina Matsuri. Houses are decorated with dolls, and rice dumplings are eaten.

Raksha Bandan is a Hindu festival where brothers and sisters show their love for each other.

This girl has made a rakhi bracelet for her brother to show how much she loves him.

Valentine's Day is on February 14th. People in many places give each other cards and presents to say "I love you."

Kwanzaa is an African-American holiday. Houses are decorated with black, red, and green streamers. People light candles and eat special food.

18

Eid-ul-Fitr is an important Muslim festival where families and friends give each other presents. Gifts of money are also given to poor people.

This girl is giving an Eid present to her sister.

Easter

Easter is celebrated by Christians all over the world. The 40-day Easter season, known as Lent, begins with a bright, colorful festival called Mardi Gras.

People make Easter bonnets and dress up for parades.

In Britain, people eat pancakes on Shrove Tuesday. Some people have pancake races and toss pancakes in the air!

On Easter Sunday, Christians go to church. They light a special candle and celebrate the day that Jesus came back to life.

Some people celebrate with Easter egg hunts and chocolate bunnies!

21

Festivals everywhere!

People all over the world enjoy festivals and celebrations! They like dressing in special clothes and costumes.

They have fun making and eating delicious festival food.

And they all enjoy parties and colorful celebrations!

What does your family celebrate?

Glossary and index

Celebrate What people do on special days, such as having a party or a parade. **4, 5**

Costume Special, decorated clothes that people wear when they are in parades and at parties. **14, 22**

Decorations Streamers, special pictures, and ornaments used to make places pretty for special days. **5, 8, 18**

Festival A time to celebrate with singing, dancing, special food, and giving thanks for the good things we have. **4, 22, 23**

Harvest The time of year when farmers collect their crops and people celebrate and give thanks for the food they have. **8, 9, 13**

Orchard Where apple trees are grown. **13**

Parade A celebration where people dress in special clothes and move down the street, singing and dancing. **20**

Succah Special tents or huts built outside by Jewish people during Succoth. **9**